Heroes Among Us

EDITED BY SARAH ARAK

Introduction

WHEN WE THINK OF HEROES, WE IMMEDIATELY CONJURE UP archetypical characteristics of physical strength, mental keenness, handsomeness, and courage. Upon closer examination, however, many less obvious qualities become apparent. Honesty, bravery, selflessness – these are just a few of the many overlooked qualities of such remarkable individuals. We think of heroes as the stuff of fairy tales, but acts of bravery can be seen in all walks of life.

Everyday heroes are individuals with great skill, courage and perseverance. They may risk or give their lives to save others, or they may dedicate their lives to improving our safety, healthcare, welfare or educational systems. Many of these remarkable individuals have given up their own comfort and/or safety in order to put others first. For this reason, our heroes deserve to be commended for the sacrifices they have made.

Heroes are real people who inspire us, by thought and example, how to live better lives. Many have themselves endured challenges, but are steadfast in their belief that goodness will overcome. Their courage and determination is awe-inspiring, and the lessons they teach stand the test of time. In good times and bad, we must take a moment to remember our unsung heroes, without whom our lives would surely be less rich.

TRUE HEROISM IS REMARKABLY SOBER, VERY UNDRAMATIC.

IT IS NOT THE URGE TO SURPASS ALL OTHERS AT

WHATEVER COST, BUT THE URGE TO

SERVE OTHERS AT WHATEVER COST.

—Arthur Ashe

WE HAVE EVERY RIGHT TO DREAM HEROIC DREAMS.

THOSE WHO SAY WE LIVE IN A TIME WHEN HEROES

DON'T EXIST, DON'T KNOW WHERE TO LOOK.

—Ronald Reagan

CONSCIENCE IS THE ROOT OF ALL TRUE COURAGE;

IF A MAN WOULD BE BRAVE, LET HIM

OBEY HIS CONSCIENCE.

—James Freeman Clarke

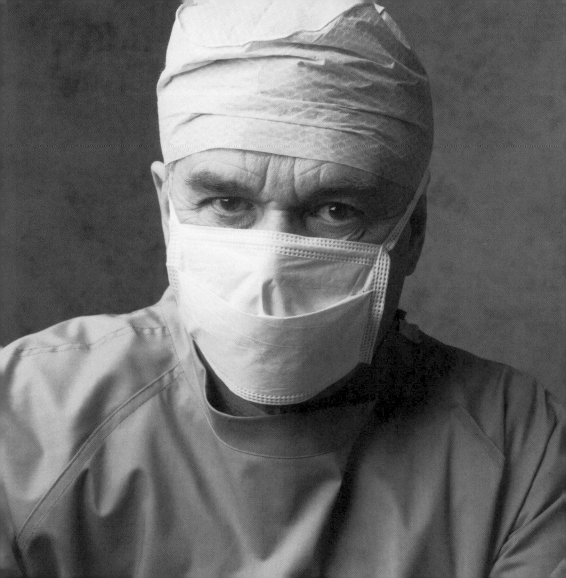

A HERO IS SOMEONE WHO HAS GIVEN

HIS OR HER LIFE TO SOMETHING

BIGGER THAN ONESELF.

— Joseph Campbell

To BE A TRUE HERO OR A HEROINE,

ONE MUST GIVE AN ORDER TO ONESELF.

—Simone Weil

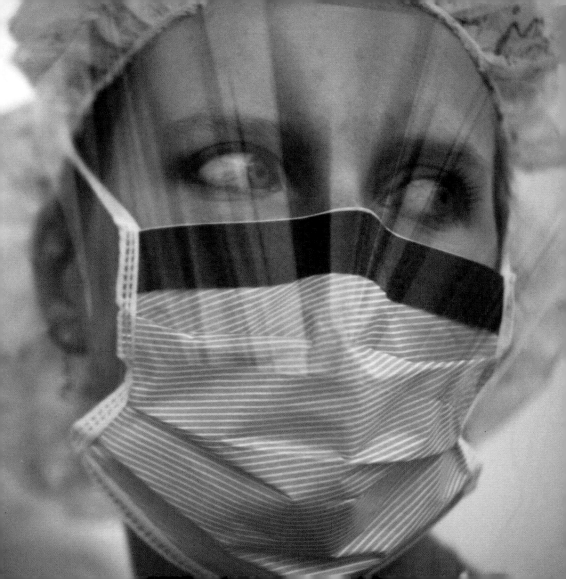

COURAGE, IT WOULD SEEM, IS NOTHING LESS THAN

THE POWER TO OVERCOME DANGER, MISFORTUNE, FEAR,

INJUSTICE, WHILE CONTINUING TO AFFIRM INWARDLY

THAT LIFE WITH ALL ITS SORROWS IS GOOD...

AND THAT THERE IS ALWAYS TOMORROW.

— Dorothy Thompson

DOWN THESE MEAN STREETS A MAN MUST GO WHO IS NOT

HIMSELF MEAN, WHO IS NEITHER TARNISHED NOR

AFRAID. HE IS THE HERO, HE IS EVERYTHING.

—Rebecca Harding Davis

HEROES MAY NOT BE BRAVER THAN ANYONE ELSE;

BUT THEY ARE BRAVER FIVE MINUTES LONGER.

—Author Unknown

Success is achievable without public recognition,

and the world has many unsung heroes.

The teacher who inspires you to pursue

your education is such a hero.

— Michael DeBakey, M.D.

THE 'AVERAGE' IS THE BORDERLINE

THAT KEEPS MERE MEN IN THEIR PLACE.

THOSE WHO STEP OVER THE LINE ARE

HEROES BY THE VERY ACT.

— Henry Rollins

THE NOIR HERO IS A KNIGHT IN BLOOD CAKED ARMOR.

HE'S DIRTY AND HE DOES HIS BEST TO DENY THE

FACT THAT HE'S A HERO THE WHOLE TIME.

— Frank Miller

Courage doesn't always roar.

Sometimes courage is the quiet voice

at the end of the day saying,

'I will try again tomorrow.'

— Mary Anne Radmacher

THE LEGACY OF HEROES IS THE MEMORY OF

A GREAT NAME AND THE INHERITANCE

OF A GREAT EXAMPLE.

— Benjamin Disraeli

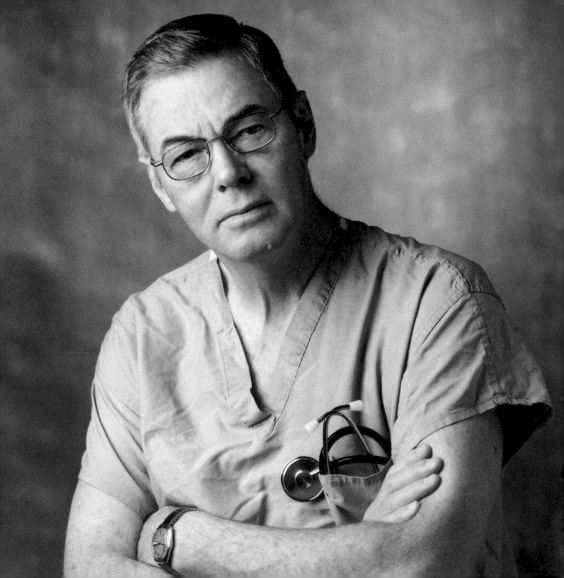

To have no heroes is to have no aspiration,

to live on the momentum of the past,

to be thrown back upon routine,

sensuality, and the narrow self.

—Charles Horton Cooley

COURAGE IS RESISTANCE TO FEAR,

MASTERY OF FEAR—NOT ABSENCE OF FEAR.

—Mark Twain

NURTURE THE MIND WITH GREAT THOUGHTS.

TO BELIEVE IN THE HEROIC MAKES HEROES.

— Benjamin Disraeli

NEVER IN THE FIELD OF HUMAN CONFLICT WAS

SO MUCH OWED BY SO MANY TO SO FEW.

— Sir Winston Churchill

THERE IS A CERTAIN ENTHUSIASM IN LIBERTY,

THAT MAKES HUMAN NATURE RISE ABOVE ITSELF,

IN ACTS OF BRAVERY AND HEROISM.

—Alexander Hamilton

COURAGE IS NOT THE ABSENCE OF FEAR,

BUT RATHER THE JUDGEMENT

THAT SOMETHING ELSE IS

MORE IMPORTANT THAN FEAR.

—Ambrose Redmoon

How IMPORTANT IT IS FOR US TO RECOGNIZE AND

CELEBRATE OUR HEROES AND SHE-ROES!

— Maya Angelou

W E COULD NEVER LEARN TO BE BRAVE

AND PATIENT IF THERE WERE

ONLY JOY IN THE WORLD.

— Helen Keller

THE ORDINARY MAN IS INVOLVED IN ACTION.

THE HERO ACTS.

AN IMMENSE DIFFERENCE.

—Henry Miller

My favorite hero is you.

WITHOUT HEROES, WE'RE ALL PLAIN PEOPLE

AND DON'T KNOW HOW FAR WE CAN GO.

— Bernard Malamud

HERE RES   IN

HONORED GL RY

AN AMERI

SOLD

KNOWN BU

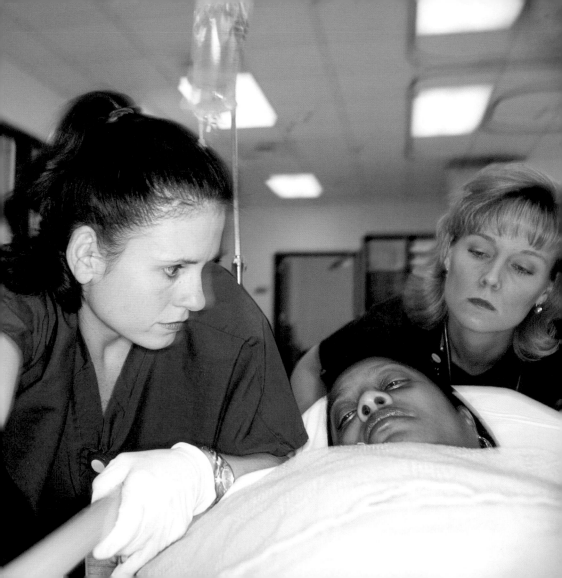

THE THING ABOUT A HERO, IS EVEN WHEN IT DOESN'T LOOK

LIKE THERE'S A LIGHT AT THE END OF THE TUNNEL,

THE HERO IS GOING TO KEEP DIGGING.

—Joss Whedon

TRUE HEROISM CONSISTS IN BEING SUPERIOR TO

THE ILLS OF LIFE, IN WHATEVER SHAPE THEY

MAY CHALLENGE US TO COMBAT.

—Napoleon Bonaparte

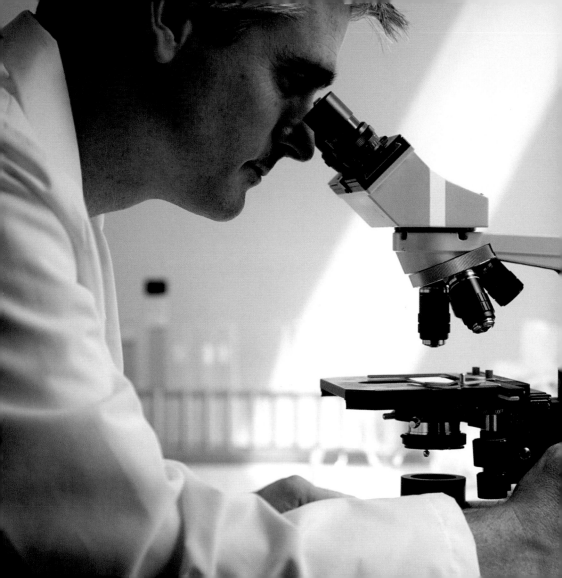

Not the glittering weapon fights the fight,

but rather the hero's heart and mind.

—Proverb

THE HERO DRAWS INSPIRATION FROM THE

VIRTUE OF HIS ANCESTORS.

—Johann Wolfgang von Goethe

THE BRAVEST ARE SURELY THOSE WHO ARE GIVEN NO

CLEAR VISION OF WHAT DANGER STANDS BEFORE THEM,

AND YET NOTWITHSTANDING, GO OUT TO MEET IT.

— Thucydides

A HERO DOESN'T HAVE TO SAVE A BUSLOAD OF

KIDS FROM CERTAIN DISASTER. OR SCORE THE WINNING POINT

IN THE BIG GAME. A HERO CAN BE ANYONE WHO INSPIRES YOU,

ANYONE YOU LOOK UP TO, ANYONE WHO CHEERS YOU ON,

MAKES YOU BETTER THAN YOU WERE BEFORE—JUST AS THEY

MADE THEMSELVES BETTER THAN THEY WERE BEFORE.

—Nike

WHEN THE WILL DEFIES FEAR, WHEN DUTY THROWS THE

GAUNTLET DOWN TO FATE, WHEN HONOR SCORNS TO

COMPROMISE WITH DEATH—THAT IS HEROISM.

—Robert Green Ingersoll

A HERO IS SOMEONE WHO UNDERSTANDS

THE RESPONSIBILITY THAT COMES

WITH HIS FREEDOM.

— Bob Dylan

WHATEVER YOU DO, YOU NEED COURAGE.

PEACE HAS ITS VICTORIES, BUT IT TAKES

BRAVE MEN AND WOMEN TO WIN THEM.

— Ralph Waldo Emerson

A HERO HAS FACED IT ALL:

HE NEED NOT BE UNDEFEATED,

BUT HE MUST BE UNDAUNTED.

— Andrew Bernstein

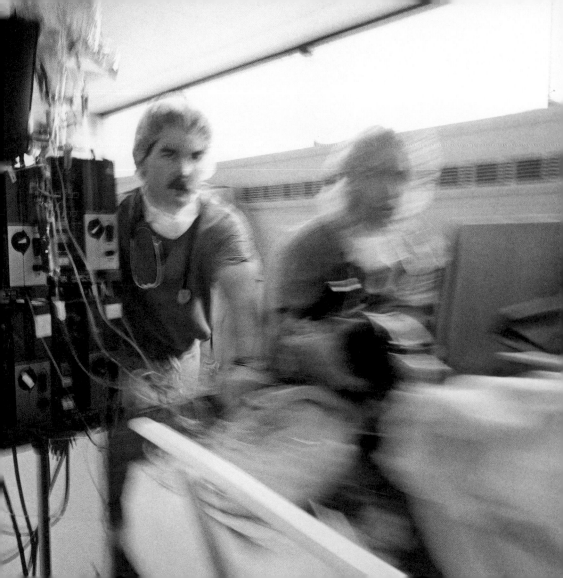

IT DOESN'T TAKE A HERO TO ORDER MEN INTO BATTLE.

IT TAKES A HERO TO BE ONE OF THOSE MEN

WHO GOES INTO BATTLE.

— Norman Schwarzkopf

A HERO IS AN ORDINARY INDIVIDUAL WHO FINDS THE

STRENGTH TO PERSEVERE AND ENDURE IN SPITE

OF OVERWHELMING OBSTACLES.

—Christopher Reeve

IT IS NOT THE CRITIC WHO COUNTS, NOT THE MAN WHO POINTS

OUT HOW THE STRONG MAN STUMBLED...THE CREDIT BELONGS

TO THE MAN WHO IS ACTUALLY IN THE ARENA, WHOSE FACE

IS MARRED BY DUST AND SWEAT AND BLOOD, WHO STRIVES

VALIANTLY, WHO ERRS AND COMES SHORT AGAIN AND AGAIN...

WHO AT BEST KNOWS ACHIEVEMENT, AND WHO AT THE WORST,

IF HE FAILS, AT LEAST FAILS WHILE DARING GREATLY.

—Theodore Roosevelt

A HERO IS A MAN WHO IS AFRAID TO RUN AWAY.

—English Proverb

Do not let the hero in your soul perish, in lonely frustration for the life you deserved, but have never been able to reach. Check your road and the nature of your battle. The world you desired can be won, it exists, it is real, it is possible; it's yours.

— Ayn Rand

THE HERO IS ONE WHO KINDLES A GREAT LIGHT IN THE WORLD,

WHO SETS UP BLAZING TORCHES IN THE DARK STREETS

OF LIFE FOR MEN TO SEE BY.

— Felix Adler

WHEN A RESOLUTE YOUNG FELLOW STEPS UP

TO THE GREAT BULLY, THE WORLD,

AND TAKES HIM BOLDLY BY THE BEARD, HE IS OFTEN

SURPRISED TO FIND IT COMES OFF IN HIS HAND,

AND THAT IT WAS ONLY TIED ON TO SCARE AWAY

THE TIMID ADVENTURERS.

—Ralph Waldo Emerson

AND SO, MY FELLOW AMERICANS:

ASK NOT WHAT YOUR COUNTRY CAN DO FOR YOU,

ASK WHAT YOU CAN DO FOR YOUR COUNTRY.

—John F. Kennedy

YOU CANNOT BELIEVE IN HONOR UNTIL

YOU HAVE ACHEIVED IT.

— George Bernard Shaw

PHOTO CREDITS